KID SCIENTIST
Volcano Experts on the Edge

Sue Fliess
illustrated by Mia Powell

Albert Whitman & Company
Chicago, Illinois

To Monique, Mark, William, and Lauren. I lava our friendship.—SF

It's a big world out there, so keep exploring!—MP

Library of Congress Cataloging-in-Publication data
is on file with the publisher.

Illustrations by Mia Powell
First published in the United States of America
in 2023 by Albert Whitman & Company
ISBN 978-0-8075-4143-2 (hardcover)
ISBN 978-0-8075-4144-9 (ebook)

Printed in China
10 9 8 7 6 5 4 3 2 1 WKT 26 25 24 23 22

Design by Mary Freelove

For more information about Albert Whitman & Company,
visit our website at www.albertwhitman.com.

“Time to meet the Queen!” Owen says to his team of volcanologists as they land in Iceland.

“But I didn’t bring my fancy clothes,” says Austin.

“Not that kind of queen,” says Katie.

Volcanologists are volcano experts—scientists who study volcanoes to learn more about their activity and behavior. Owen's team has come to research the Herdubreid (HAIR-the-breth) volcano. But locals have another name for the volcano...

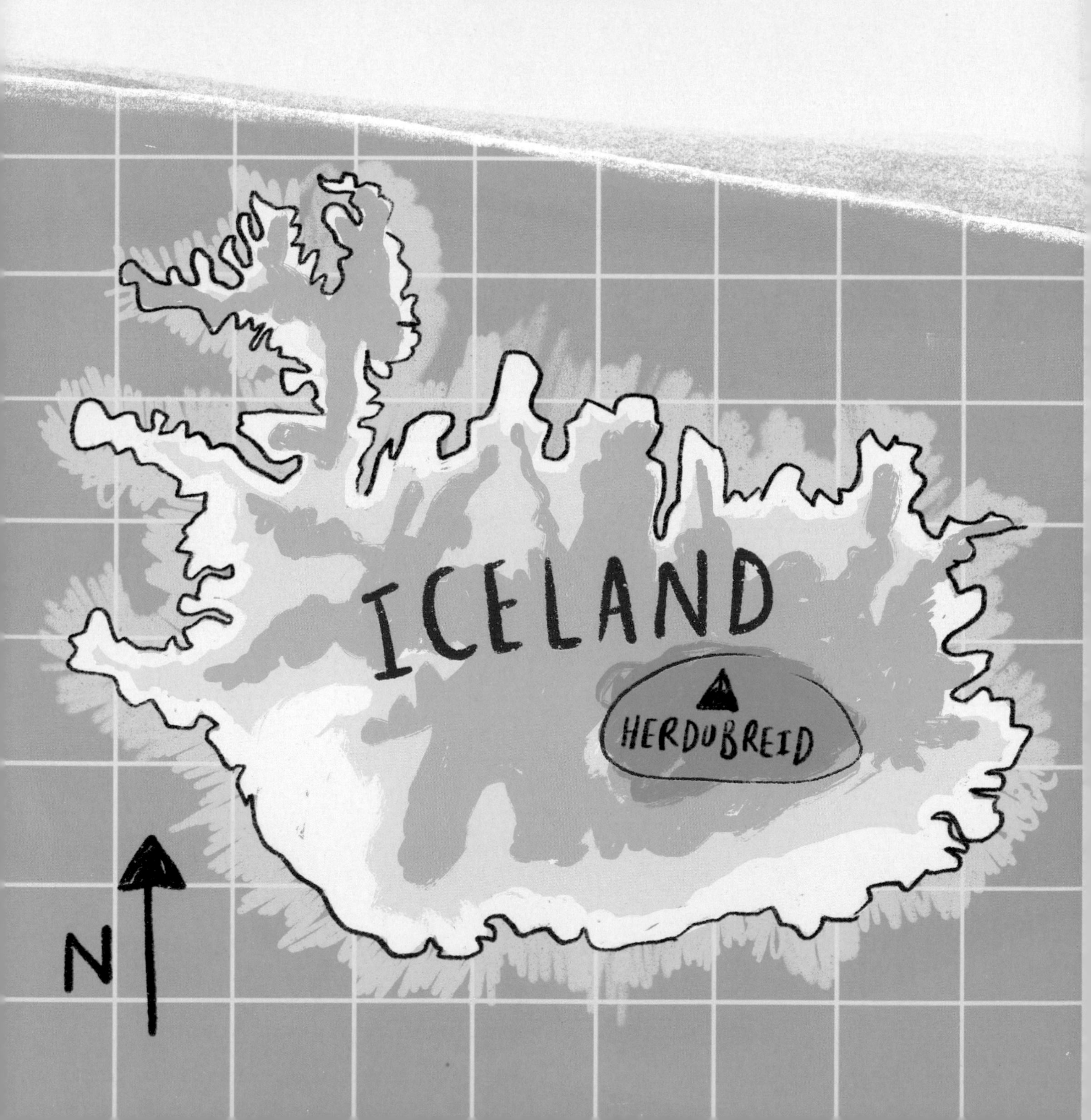

“They call it the Queen of Icelandic Mountains because it resembles a crown,” says Owen. “It last erupted over 10,000 years ago, during the most recent ice age, so it’s dormant. That means it’s stopped erupting—for now.”

“Even dormant volcanoes can erupt again,” says Austin.

“That’s why we’re here to study it,” says Owen. “To find out if there’s any chance for more volcanic activity.”

Owen shares his hypothesis, or guess based on research, with his team. "I believe the Queen is actually *extinct*, meaning it will never erupt again."

"If that's true, Icelanders will be happy to know the volcano isn't dangerous anymore," says Austin.

"When volcanoes have erupted here in the past, the ash and gases they spewed have made people more than one hundred miles away sick," says Katie.

The team drives for many hours before reaching a field of rocks formed from past volcanic eruptions. Looking up, the scientists know the trip was worth it.

"Incredible," says Owen. "I can see why they call it the Queen."

The team sets up a station where they can discuss their findings, store their instruments, and sleep at night.

"To find out if the Queen is extinct, we'll need to learn if it has been cut off from its magma, or hot melted rock, supply," says Owen. "If magma has built up, it will have created pressure inside the volcano. When too much pressure builds, the volcano erupts."

“Thankfully we’ve brought plenty of tools that can tell us if an eruption is likely,” says Katie.

“Let’s get to work!” says Austin.

The three scientists grab their hiking poles, backpacks, and tools and start to climb the volcano.

"Watch your step," says Owen as he tightens his helmet. "There's scree, or loose rocks formed from past rockfalls, which can make it easy to slip and fall."

“Our hiking poles can help us,” says Katie. “They’re like an extra set of legs.”

“I wish I really did have an extra set of legs,” says Austin. “This is hard work!”

After several hours, the team finally reaches the top.

"Awesome!" says Owen, looking down into the bowl-shaped top of the volcano.

"It's amazing to think this whole crater was formed by an eruption, all those years ago," says Katie.

"Feels like we're on top of the world!" says Austin.

Katie examines large rocks with her hand lens, which magnifies objects to ten times their actual size. She chips off pieces of rock with a hammer and places them in her backpack to study back at the station.

Owen takes out a ground-based sensor. "This device sends out signals to measure movement in the ground. If my hypothesis is correct and the volcano is extinct, there shouldn't be any movement."

Austin gets a drone ready for flying. “I’m going to study the land around the volcano. The drone’s camera can take photos and videos that will help me make a 3D map of the volcano. We can also use the drone to test Owen’s hypothesis.”

“That’s right,” says Owen. “The drone is carrying a gas-sniffing device that can measure levels of sulfur dioxide and carbon dioxide coming from the volcano. Volcanoes emit these gases when they’re active, so if there isn’t any gas coming out, it will support my hypothesis that the volcano is extinct.”

“Look at it soar!” says Austin.

After collecting samples and taking measurements, the team heads down the volcano.

“Did you know that astronauts can see large volcanic eruptions from space?” Austin asks his teammates.

“And that satellites orbiting Earth use radar to measure shifts in mountainsides?” Owen adds.

“We can check the Queen’s satellite data later,” says Katie. “If the mountainside hasn’t shifted, that will help prove the volcano is extinct.”

At the station the next morning, the team reviews their findings.

"One of the rocks I collected is part of a lava plug," says Katie. "It's made of the hardened magma that cooled and blocked the Queen's vent."

"What does that mean for our research?" asks Austin.

"It may support Owen's hypothesis," says Katie. "This volcano's lava plug is heavily eroded, or worn down. That could mean the volcano hasn't had liquid magma inside of it in a long, long time."

The team checks the data they've collected to further test Owen's hypothesis.

"The satellite data shows the mountainside has not shifted," says Katie.

"And the gas-sniffing device on the drone doesn't show any gas emissions," says Austin.

"Just one more system to check," says Owen as he reads the ground sensor's measurements. "The sensors didn't measure any movement under the volcano either. This means there's no magma building up below the Queen. Together, all our findings show that this volcano is officially extinct!"

“Usually, I wouldn’t cheer about extinction,” says Katie, “but now the people of Iceland can know that this volcano will never cause any damage again.”

The team will write up a full report of their results to share with other volcanologists.

Just then, they hear Owen from outside the tent. "Austin, Katie, come quick!"

"Could we have been wrong?" asks Austin. "Could the volcano be erupting?"

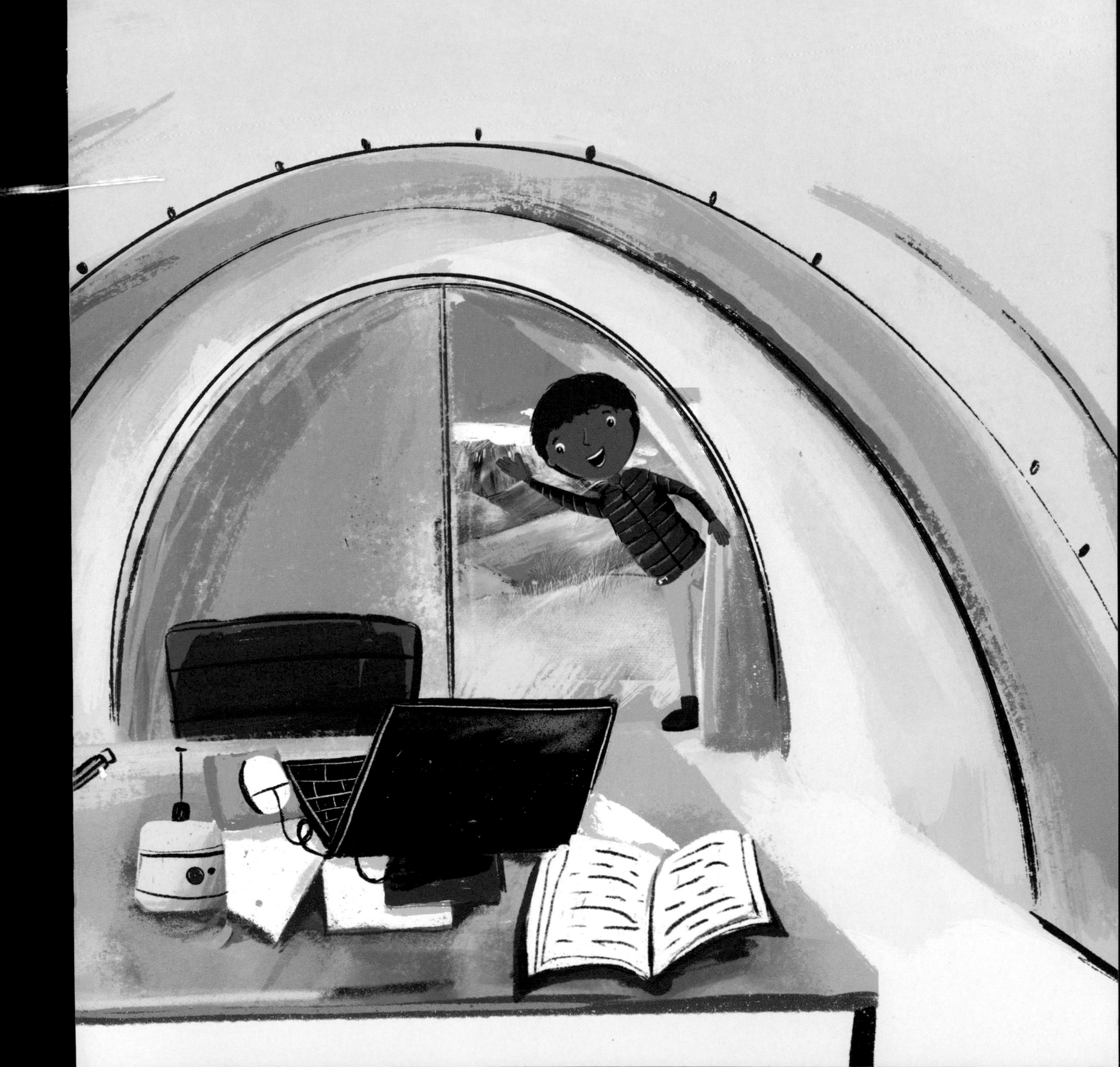

When they go outside, they see Owen standing by a helicopter.

"Surprise!" he says. "We're going to see the Queen from the air to *royally* appreciate her."

“The Queen can finally rest,” says Katie.

Owen waves as they leave the volcano behind. “See you later, Your Majesty!”

WHAT IS A VOLCANOLOGIST?

Volcanology, a branch of geology, is the study of volcanoes, which are openings in Earth's crust where melted rock and hot gases come to the surface—sometimes loudly and forcefully and sometimes quietly. Volcanologists are scientists who seek to understand how volcanoes work and behave to predict future eruptions for the safety of local populations. To do their jobs, they travel to volcanoes and set up stations around them where they keep their tools and gear and often stay while doing their research. They also work in labs, where they document their work.

Volcanologists use many different instruments to detect and record earthquakes, measure changes to volcanoes' surfaces, detect and measure volcanic gases, and determine how much lava is moving underground. These instruments include drones; video, still, and infrared cameras; satellite imagers; and more.

All scientists conduct research by following the steps of the scientific method. Owen and his team used each step to guide their research.

STEPS OF THE SCIENTIFIC METHOD

1. Make observations and do background research. Before Owen and his team traveled to Iceland, they did research on the Herdubreid volcano.
2. Ask questions about your observations and gather information. Knowing that the Herdubreid volcano was dormant, Owen wondered if the volcano would ever erupt again. He asked about ground movement and gas emissions from the mountain.
3. Form a hypothesis. After learning that the activity on the volcano had slowed down, Owen formed a hypothesis that the Herdubreid volcano was not only dormant, but also extinct.
4. Perform an experiment and collect data. Owen and his team gathered data from the volcano by setting up ground sensors to detect movement of magma. They also flew a drone with a gas-sniffer to measure gas emissions.
5. Analyze the data and draw conclusions. Consider how the conclusions support or disprove your hypothesis. Once the team had a chance to examine the volcano and collect data, they were able to conclude that there was no movement of magma, and no detection of gas emissions or shifts in the mountain. All of this supported Owen's hypothesis that the volcano was extinct.
6. Communicate or present your findings. After gathering their data, Owen and his team will publish their research to inform the scientific community that the volcano is officially extinct and explain how they arrived at that conclusion.

HOW CAN I BECOME A VOLCANOLOGIST?

Volcanologists usually have advanced degrees in geology and are trained to use scientific equipment to gather data. If you're curious about how and why volcanoes erupt, maybe you'll become a volcanologist!

There are many ways to study what goes on in the earth, even before you decide on a career.

- Check out books on geology or volcanology at your local library.
- If you can, take a tour of a mine to learn about the different types of rocks and minerals in the earth.
- Take a nature hike and bring a magnifying glass to look closely at rocks.
- If you ever go on vacation in a place with volcanoes, try to visit one.

When you're older, you can choose a college that offers a degree in geology or geoscience. There are many specialties that can be used in volcanology, including geology, geophysics, geochemistry, biology, biochemistry, mathematics, statistics, engineering, atmospheric science, and remote sensing. To become a volcanologist, you'll need an advanced degree in geology or geoscience. But if you have a bachelor's degree, you can still work as an assistant or a technician.

Volcanologists need skills in communication, science, and computers. They must be able to hike long distances and work and live outdoors for extended periods. In the United States, many volcanologists work for the US Geological Survey or as professors at universities. Maybe you'll even join the Geological Society of America!

SUGGESTED READING FOR KIDS

Howell, Izzi. *Volcano Geo Facts*. New York: Crabtree, 2018.

McGlone, Catherine. *Visiting Volcanoes with a Scientist*. Berkeley Heights, NJ: Enslow, 2004.

Nargi, Lela, and Arianna Soldati. *Volcanoes*. Washington, DC: National Geographic, 2018.